Spiritual Law

A Handbook to Higher Truth

Cover Design by C.J. Kershner

Spiritual Law

A Handbook to Higher Truth

Elaine Bartlett

Daystar Direct
1994

"And He who knew and brought me up
is the Most High in all His perfection.
And He glorified me by His kindness,
and raised my thoughts to the height of his Truth.
And from thence He gave me the way
of His precepts and I opened the doors
that were closed."

Ode 17:7-10

Dedication

This work is dedicated to the Supreme Law Maker
and to my brothers and sisters
as we strive to remember,
"I Am the Law made manifest."

And to my beloved son, Robert,
who holds the candle
which lights up my life.

Acknowledgments

This book has been lovingly guided by unseen Forces. I trust my thoughts of gratitude are carried Home. The extraordinary wisdom of Melchizedek and the Ancient Tibetan are acknowledged as well as the words of Gabriel.

Mother, my personal earth Angel, you taught me to treasure every moment as a gift from God and to put my time to good use. Bill, Martha, Julia and Janel, where would the joy have been in this lifetime without you. And Dad, even from your perch on High, you made me double check everything! In your uniqueness, you are each loved dearly.

Sandy Cotton, your friendship and loyalty over the years are among the greatest of gifts the Father has given me. Jim De Armond, without you the laws would not have come to light.
Linda and Ron Sklar, thank you for being here.

The many friends and students who have staunchly persevered until I could see the laws clearly enough to bring them into focus, thank you for teaching me.

Appearing as earth Angels, so many of you have touched me deeply over the years. I hope to return your love by sharing my simple understanding of these ancient truths.

And finally, my Guardian Angel. Did you realize there would be so much overtime with this case when you signed on? Thank you.

My love enfolds each of you.

Introduction

Engraved in the depths of each soul, in the Holy of Holies where the conscience dwells, is a set of rules, a code of behavior of Divine origin, by which we must live.

When we become sufficiently silent and sufficiently humble to hear the still small voice of the LAW within, and have the courage to follow it at all time, we will fulfill our destiny and become what we are created to be - God in action.

These rules are known as Spiritual Laws or Principles and they form the framework of our Universe. By virtue of these LAWS, the Universe exists and is held together. Considered Absolute, they govern this plane and every other plane and dimension of reality. As Infinite, nothing confines or restricts the law other than the LAW itself. These Principles cannot be increased or diminished as they are Immutable. And, they are Eternal; they exist out of time, without beginning or end.

The Spiritual Laws are designed to facilitate our realization, recognition and manifestation of our indwelling God. It is time to remove our blinders and embrace the inner Laws which hold the secret to our happiness. We must take responsibility and look within to rediscover the rhythm of natural balance. We took a physical form to demonstrate the Spiritual Laws.

"As soon as one acknowledges the Light of Self as his true guide, and with undying love that neither rests nor hastes, works with the Law, he attracts in virtue of his striving all the affinities corresponding to his own nature from the higher spheres, and on the fruitful foundation of these affinities he mounts upwards to the Great Fountain of Eternal Truth."
   * Mysteries of the Qabalah

While residing on Earth we agreed, at some level of consciousness, to honor the law of the land and, so, we must. Man-made laws, however, are limited in scope and duration and pertain only to a finite world.

YOU ARE INFINITE! YOU ARE A SPIRITUAL BEING "ENJOYING" A HUMAN EXPERIENCE. As such, you are bound and guided by your inner Spiritual Law. LAW lets your spirit soar. Recognize and honor your LAW and you become the master of your destiny.

The infinite number of laws are but various depictions of the One Great Law "I AM ALL." Nothing exists outside this LAW and nothing happens contrary to it. YOU can never be outside the LAW because THE LAW IS YOU.

"The word "Lord"in Holy Scripture, should be LAW, for the Lord of God is in reality and in truth, the LAW of God. It is not the physical being, as is commonly accepted by the orthodox individual because of translations."
   * Ancient Mystical White Brotherhood

In the Instruction Manual issued when embarking upon this earthly adventure, we were told, "Love the Lord your God with your whole heart." Substitute the word LAW for Lord and the real meaning surfaces. Love the LAW your God with your whole heart.

In simple terms, the LAW is within -
love it and you LOVE YOURSELF.

It is then easy to love everything else.

The words "I AM" are the acknowledgment and release of the power to create and bring forth ideas into expression. The thought or spoken word of "I AM" arouses the creative energy instantly. We become what we say or believe.

Live the Spirit of the LAW rather than the letter.
It is Infinitely Lighter!

As we learn and live our LAW, doors we only dimly remember will swing open. Once again, we will find our selves in the garden of Eden.

Love the LAW and walk through the Door.

This work has been inspired by THE SUPREME LAW MAKER with the promise wherever you open this book, the LAW which can most benefit you will surface. At this particular juncture in your life, the LAW you select has a deep and holy message. The God in you drew the LAW unto Itself. Trust.

"I AM" THE LAW

I COME TO FULFILL THE LAW

"I AM" YOU

YOU AND I ARE ONE

YOU ARE DEMONSTRATING THE LAW
AT ALL TIMES

AND THE LAW IS.....

ABUNDANCE

Opulence is your Divine birthright!

Wealth of body, mind and spirit
is yours for the claiming.

To collect this rightful inheritance of Abundance,
recognize all wealth is WITHIN you. Know you are
created in RICHNESS and FULLNESS and this law
will successfully demonstrate itself in your world.

Deficiency is rooted in "poor" consciousness.

Do not cling to poverty thoughts. Nurturing ideas
contrary to the Law of Abundance erodes
your ability to manifest your dreams.

Fear not! Your every need is amply met.

The essence of you overflows with Abundance.

In the Mind of God THERE IS NO LACK.

ADORATION

"Glorify thou Me, the One Whom I AM,
for I AM ALL, and no other is." *

Have profound reverence and respect for the Source
of all Life. You are ordained to love in the highest
degree possible by adoring and glorifying the Light.

"What I AM thou art, for thou art ME;
thou art the whole." *

The Source of Light resides within yourself.
Honor this One, Central, Higher Power.

Discover and adore the Light
within each person, place or thing.

The whole demands adoration
as does each and every part.

* The Divine Iliad

AFFINITY

Affinity is the force which binds atom to atom,
cell to cell and concept to concept.
An incubation period then follows for the nurturing,
building, and duplicating of atom, cell or concept
until the respective form is manifested.

Changing from state to state, degree by degree,
condition to condition, pole to pole, vibration to
vibration, gradually establishes and defines
that toward which you hold an affinity.

For example, if you have a sweet tooth but know it is
time to enjoy a more wholesome diet, Affinity sets
the pace for change. Degree by degree, (bite by bite)
as allegiance is shifted,
a taste for more nourishing food is cultivated.

Don't gulp life.
Savor each forkful.
When you acquire a taste for something new,
ask for another menu.

ALCHEMY

You have the power to transmute
every circumstance in your life.
Actually, it is your obligation to change
and lighten up.

You are the magician
cradling the cup which holds the elixir of life.

Exchange low, base, undesirable thoughts
and actions for more noble ideals and deeds.

Unleash your power.

Dissolve that which no longer serves
the Master Magician.

Melt your beingness into pure gold.

ALL IS IN ALL

"All is in THE ALL;
it is equally true that THE ALL is in All."*

Every part of the whole
is contained in the very least of molecules.
The very least of molecules
is entirely in the whole.

NOTHING exists outside THE ALL.
Otherwise, All would not be THE ALL!

* Hermetic Principle

AS ABOVE,
SO BELOW

AS BELOW,
SO ABOVE

There is correspondence,
harmony and agreement between the laws
and the phenomena of the various
planes of being and life.

An inter-dependency exists between all levels
and types of existence,
including life forms beyond our current awareness
and recognition.

The same laws and characteristics apply to each unit
or combination of units, while each manifests
its own phenomena on its individual plane.

As a charter member of the Cosmic family,
you move as a whole, integrated group.
When one suffers, all suffer;
when one is exalted, all are elevated.

ASKING

"Ask and it shall be given you;
Seek, and ye shall find;
Knock and it shall be opened." Matt. 7:7

Speak up. Make your wishes known.
A petition sets Divine Energy in motion.

Be precise!
Clearly define your aims and goals,
hopes and wishes.

Hold firmly to that which you seek.
Do not give up knocking -
even when your knuckles buckle!

NO ASK .... NO GET!

NO SEEK .... NO FIND!

NO KNOCK......... NO REPLY!

AS WITHIN,
SO WITHOUT

AS WITHOUT,
SO WITHIN

I behold that which I am.

We see things not as they are but as we are,

ALWAYS.

ATTRACTION

You are a living magnet.

Persons and situations gravitate to or are repelled
from you based on the pitch and proportion of your
deepest beliefs and feelings.

You pull to yourself that which is OF yourself at some
level of reality. For better or worse, like does attract
like.

All things manifesting in your life
are there because you magnetized them
at some stage of your evolution.

The power to attract transcends this particular plane
of existence. Upon making the decision to take a
human body, a spirit is drawn into a vortex of energy
that corresponds to the energy signals emanating
from the "creators" at the climax of the act.

Highly evolved beings of Light wait in the wings to
populate the earth.
Attract these radiant souls
with the intensity and power of Love.

BALANCE

"When man thinketh Me in him,
then is man's balance absolute."*

You are a crystalline channel
for the perfect expression of poise and harmony.

Develop and nourish body, mind and spirit
simultaneously.

Focus of attention to one body, to the detriment
of the others, eventually creates an imbalance
throughout the system.

Weigh in on the scale of Rhythmic Balance.
It's the Way In.

* The Divine Iliad

BEAUTY

See with the Eye of Beauty
and you see with the Eye of God.

Behold the underlying splendor
which is present in everyone and everything.

Delight in the magnificence of your own soul
and you will easily discern
the beauty inherent in all creation.

BLESSING

Mentally anoint all persons and circumstances
in your life to invoke the goodness
buried within their essence.

Bless it and it blesses you; curse it and it curses you.

A widespread epidemic of "cursing" now rages
through society. Mindlessly, humans chant
the refrain, "another damn day." Persons carelessly
"damn" family and friends, job or lot in life.

The litany of curses is endless
with little or no effort put forth to counter the
negativity by calling upon the Law of Blessing.

All things are a blessing.
BLESS equally the good, the bad, and the ugly!

Your investment of constructive energy
will yield hefty dividends.

BREATH

The main object of the game of life
is to stay in it!

As you consciously or subconsciously curtail
the breathing pattern, ever so subtly,
the valve of life closes. Enthusiasm, creativity
and energy seemingly evaporate.

The physical, mental and spiritual bodies respond
to the depth and rhythmic measure of Breath.

Depression, pessimism and negativity rob
these bodies of oxygen. Eventually various physical
organs deteriorate giving way to a sagging, drooping
body; a pathetic testimony to violation
of the Law of Breath.

Every deep in-breath fills the organs
with power and energy; out-breath releases
fear and toxins from the body.

Stand straight! Breathe deeply!
Breath is Life - Choose Life.

COMMUNICATION

Interchange of thought, word or feeling allows
the illusion of separateness to diminish while
the perception of Oneness expands.

Get in touch with yourself.
Listen to your intuition.
This is your Higher Self clamoring for an audience!

Cells of the body communicate with one another.
Use this knowledge to spread light and healing
inside your physical structure.

All universes thrive on sharing and participation.

Physically, mentally and spiritually you have ready
access to communicate with the mineral, plant,
animal and Angel kingdoms. You are free to connect
with spirit guides and ancient teachers. Friends
and loved ones on various astral dimensions await
your attention to share insights and knowledge.

Use your credit card or dial direct, but phone Home!

COMMUNION

COMMUNION

The gentle beat of your heart lovingly guides you to commune with those beings that already live in your soul.

Embrace the intimacy of sharing your thoughts and feelings with a kindred spirit.

COMPASSION

Evoke tenderness and empathy for all
so that you no longer hold others
as separate and distinct from yourself.

Opening to the plight of another
expands your Realization of Oneness.

Act now.

COMPENSATION

Measure for measure, the equivalent
of your every thought, word and deed returns to you.
Input out = output in!

In certain cultures an exchange of currency
is an appropriate means of compensation for goods,
knowledge or services rendered. In other parts
of the world, exchange of time, talent or wisdom
is the suitable way to restore the balance of energy.

Allow the good you do to return to you;
avoid imbalance accruing upon
the scale of fairness.

If you have harmed another life form in thought
or action, you must make amends. Replace or restore
the equivalent of what was taken, damaged or lost.

Settle up honorably if you wish to be settled UP.

CONCENTRATION

Focus and direct energy with intensity. Be passionate.
Develop laser-sharp attention.

When an idea begins to take shape,
moving toward becoming a creation,
zealously project enthusiasm and determination.
Be single-minded.

Center on ONE thing at a time.
Bring it to a point of completion and perfection.

Results will materialize as originally envisioned.

Then, on to the next great adventure.

CONSECRATION

Dedicate all circumstances, situations
and predicaments to God.

This simple act of dedication burns away the dross
from the apparently less-than-perfect experience
and heightens every other experience.

.

CORRESPONDENCE

Your essence contains that which is equivalent to
and in perfect harmony with
all that is above and all that is below
on the evolutionary scale.*

There is an interconnection between the laws
and phenomena of the various planes of existence.
Occurrences and events in the dimensions above
transpire in equal ratio on the planes below
and vice versa. Indeed, a single thought affects
life forms on every dimension.

Mortal reasoning can conceive of the monad
and thus understand the Archangel.
From the known, one deduces the Unknown.

* Hermetic Principle

COURAGE

COURAGE

The Law of Courage enables one to face hardships
and tragedies with resoluteness and determination.

Bravery becomes the instrument
through which the heart center
is activated and opened.

Love from the heart -- heartily!

CREATION

Earth is a university for creators-in-training.
In this hall of learning, souls master
the art of sculpting as aims, goals, hopes and wishes
take form and acquire texture.

Thought and emotion trigger the creative process;
manifestation thrives on clarity.
Constructive creativity knows no boundaries;
use your imagination.

Graduate with honors.

CYCLES

Cycles afford individuals and universes
opportunity for "upward mobility."

The rhythmic inhaling and exhaling
of the Solar Logos causes expansion and contraction,
moving star systems and their inhabitants
in a spiral pattern.

At the present time, on a universal level,
three major cycles are enfolding
to a season of closure.
Light, love and power are pulsing toward us
as we move into a wondrous new phase.
The earth and all her children
are involved in this shift.

We are undergoing a time of purification as
we prepare to access the wonders
of the next stage of our evolution.

DESIRE

Desire to be the Light You Are.

The Sun has dawned.
Avail yourself of ITS tremendous power.

De-sire means "down from the Father."
Step down this Divine Energy.
Bring heaven into YOUR earth.

Truly, anything your heart desires can come to you.

DISCERNMENT

Perceive truth based upon "IN-sight".

Use inner vision to discern the validity of that which is
sensed and experienced.
Employ the All-Knowing Eye (I) of Love and Wisdom
for infallible deductions.

Observe one another's differences yet know
Truth is a Rainbow of Energy,
a spectrum of beliefs and ideas,
each permeated with a measure of Light.

DOOR LAW

"When a door closes,
a window opens." *

Trust the Force that closed the door in the first place!

*Irish Proverb

ENERGY

Energy IS the Life Force in action,
contemplation or stillness.
All the power you need is always available to you.

Wasting energy by a negative approach to life
is not energy efficient.
Depression or repression, anger or fear drain
the reservoir, leaving you depleted of vim and vigor,
wondering if someone pulled the plug
on the Divine Pool of Energy.

You have unlimited reserves of Energy.
Go with the flow in mind, body and spirit.
Cultivate a constructive, positive approach to life.
Endless Energy will surge to restore
and recharge your battery.

ENTHUSIASM

Enthusiasm sparks Energy.
Energy ignites Ecstasy.

Enthusiasm kindles the Life Spark by unleashing
awesome forces of creative energy.
Electricity is actually charged, recharged
and then discharged.

The fire of enthusiasm is stoked
when you choose joy;
energy explodes into ecstasy.

Ecstasy gloriously inflames your godliness.

EQUALITY

"All is in THE ALL, THE ALL is in All.
I AM one and the same in All." *

I AM the same root cause in everyone and everything.
Nothing and no one is greater or less,
superior or inferior, better or worse.

In Essence, there is no separation
and there is no difference. The qualifying essence
(that which makes anything as it is) of both
manifested and unmanifested universes,
is the Life Force.
This Force moves impartially
and evenly throughout all.

* Hermetic Principle

EVOLUTION

The nature of Life Itself is to unfold,
open and expand.

The Law of Evolution challenges each individual
spark of the Godhead to disentangle itself
from the constraints of limited thinking.

As a soul gradually evolves,
an expanded awareness of the Higher Self dawns.
The spirit takes wings and upgrades consciousness
to First Class Status.

Enjoy the flight. Lighten up!

EXPANSION

Recognize the kingdom of God within
for the explicit purpose of expanding and opening
the Higher Self out from Its center.

The God essence of you was born to stretch!

In the higher realms, everything which is created
immediately begins to expand into greater
and greater service and perfection.
On this plane, human creations often originate
from a base of fear, greed, lust or revenge;
decay sets in almost upon inception of the work.

Take command of the thought process,
widen your horizons.
Expend effort and energy with discernment.
Ideas must be permeated with unconditional love
to derive long-lasting results.

Leave an indelible mark
benefiting this world and all other universes.

EXPECTANCY

YOU GET EXACTLY WHAT YOU EXPECT,
nothing more, nothing less.

Thoughts are charged with electricity.
A magnetic force field is established by the soul
as it consciously or unconsciously affirms
that which it is envisioning.
As the vision grows, for better or worse,
the results becomes more concrete.

Often expectations are established based on
ignorance or fear. Insist on expecting the worst
and you won't be disappointed.

Why not expect the best?
What about a miracle or two?
After all, in your divinity, you are a miracle worker.

FAITH

Faith embraces an affirmative mental approach
to life as opposed to a negative one.
A positive attitude or act on your part
prompts a beneficent act of God.

Take the initiative, embrace Faith.
The God being of your soul will take over from there.

Believe in yourself. Cultivate self-reliance.
Through times of doubt, get a better grip.
Listen intently to the one, true, Inner Voice
as the source of direction and guidance.

In Faith, follow directions.
The road will be made easy.
You will not be disappointed.

FEARLESSNESS

Fear is any "mental road trip" under-taken without packing the awareness of the ever-present Presence. It is the opposite pole of Fearlessness.

The idea of something "other" than the central force of good as the controlling element, grabs hold of the soul and paralyzes it. Fear taunts and threatens its victims with an impending sense of doom, dread, and danger wreacking havoc within the life plan.

KNOW the guiding Force IS operating.
Be brave. Nothing can hurt you.
"No harm can come near your tent!" *

* 91st Psalm

FORGIVENESS

In order to grow, one must give up
negative attitudes and worn-out thought patterns
and habits for that which is higher and brighter.

"For-give" signals an opportunity
to "give up old for new."

GIVE IT UP!

Go beyond what the five senses dictate as real.
Look, listen and understand with the eye of love.
That which you do is done with the amount of Light
you choose to use at that time.

With more Light you would do things differently.
Turn your Light on.

Trapped in the belief that someone or something
outside yourself is responsible
for your lack of happiness or well-being?
The seed of discord rests in you. LET IT GO.
How often do you proudly proclaim,
"I forgive, but I won't forget!"
If you have not forgotten,
YOU HAVE NOT FORGIVEN.

Procure a new lease on life.
Release to re-lease!

FREEDOM

In ancient Sanskrit, "free" means to love and "dom"
means law (lord), power or jurisdiction.

Combine "free" and "dom" for the true message:
Love the lord of your being
and you grasp the scepter of power and jurisdiction
over all circumstances in life.
This is Freedom.

Souls choose this earthly dimension to learn
and appreciate the value of serving; however,
if oppression or repression become the instructors,
the Law of Freedom has been distorted.

Regardless of appearance, each soul
is without restraint or constriction.
Freedom is often abused, compromised or neglected,
yet the Spirit of Freedom prevails
throughout all turmoil.

Treasure the sacredness of your freedoms,
Enlightenment rides upon her wings.

FULFILLMENT

God is whole and complete.
Every thought or action ever stirred into existence
MUST come to completion or fruition.
Hence, whatsoever YOU set in motion is fulfilled.

Since nothing God creates can be incomplete,
create with care, god. If you exclaim, for instance,
"I am sick and tired of...", this becomes your law.
As the nature of this precept is completion,
the decree fulfills itself and you become
that which you declared -- sick and tired. Nice job!

Watch your mouth.
Honor your word.
Keep commitments and promises.

Guarantee yourself a grand finale.

GENDER

The Universe is comprised of a perfectly balanced
ratio of positive and negative energy.
Gender exists in equal proportion of masculine
and feminine energy in all things and on all planes.

Collectively, we are opening to the essentialness
of balancing the male/female aspects of our nature.
Men, while retaining the powerful positive qualities of
their nature, must awaken the sensitive faculties
of intuition, understanding, and empathy.
Women must preserve their femininity and sensitivity
while simultaneously arousing the positive,
assertive side of their nature.
Intelligence and sound reasoning must be tempered
with tenderness and kindness
in men and women alike.

The balancing of yin and yang,
a harmonizing of right and left brain activity,
is mandatory.

Discover and revere both halves of your divinity;
you make a perfect whole!

GRACE

Grace broadcasts a subtle frequency renewing
the heart center and intoning the spirit
with a knowingness that it is ALWAYS under
the favor and protection
of the Head of the broadcasting company.

Through the beneficence of pardon and mercy,
divine energy is ceaselessly emitted,
ever moving you into a state of reconciliation
with the God essence of your being.

HARMLESSNESS

Choose to consciously live in a state of innocence,
inwardly harboring no malice or injurious thoughts
toward another - including yourself.

Thought, with the intent to perpetrate harm against
another person, place or thing,
damages to lesser or greater extent that
toward which the thought was directed.
Unfortunately for the perpetrator,
the entire proposition backfires returning
the negative energy to the sender fast and furiously.
Hardly worth the energy!

The best defense is no defense.
The best offense is "inoffense."
Disarm your need to harm. NOW!

HARMONY

You are a glorious living symphony!
All of the notes and chords of this magnificent
orchestration must be played in balanced rhythm
and resonate to the base note of your being, Light.

Discover your own special keynote
and allow it free, full expression.
Play your tune to perfection.
Become a Maestro in the symphony of the Spheres.

HEALTH

Buried deep within each cell is the fundamental
memory of its true nature– whole, complete
and perfect. The system continually restores itself
to its basic pattern, the one REALITY, perfect health.
It is sabotaged frequently.

You are designed to be in perfect working order.

As a three-part being (body, mind and spirit), each
must be fully functioning to bypass the imbalance
which eventually results in health disorders.

Disease is the result of your own dis-ease.
It is not the random act of some distant god.

When illness arises, wisdom nudges you to search
for the underlying cause of your discomfort
and dis-ease.
The body has agreed, at an unconscious level,
to absorb the brunt of the experience
hoping you will clearly see the effects of unhealthy
thought or action and work to restore balance.

Take responsibility for your less-than-perfect creation.
What you have created can be recreated.
This is part of your job description.

Healing is a decision to return to Truth →
"I AM WHOLE, COMPLETE AND PERFECT."

HOPE

Reach out with your desires
ever holding an awareness of the Presence
as the motivating force.

Strive for fulfillment of your wishes.
Search for and expect the good
which Hope promises.

I AM

"I AM, therefore, nothing else is. I AM ALL.
I AM IN ALL THINGS.
I AM WITHIN, WITHOUT. I AM ALL IN ALL.
I AM; I ALONE AM." *

Knowledge of the "I AM" principle
is embedded in the center of your being.

It is your job to actualize this knowingness.
Yet, to know It, you must desire to know It.

When you KNOW, you BECOME — "I AM THAT I AM."

* Divine Iliad

INTEGRITY

Remind your body, mind and spirit
that it is ONE, integrated being.

Honor it. Respect it.

Attune to the highest principles within yourself.
The results are purely wholesome!

INTELLIGENCE

Intellect reasons.
Intelligence KNOWS.

Intelligence is not an IQ score.
Intelligence is a remembering of true identity.

Seek the divine Intelligence present in all life forms.

INTUITION

You have unlimited ability to access, understand
and apply information pulsating from any dimension
throughout the universe.

Put reason aside. Feel! Sense!

Forcing Intuition to yield Her secrets through drugs
or other dangerous substances and practices
is not only dangerous, but potentially deadly.
Progress screeches to a temporary halt.

Heightened perceptions are most easily
and safely attained by refining dietary habits
and moderate fasting.
Also, try prayer or meditation.

A universal network of information swirls about you.
Perk up your antenna
and experience clear reception and fine transmission.

JOY

Learn to laugh. More.
Let the silver lining of your silly-side shine.

Experience elevation and exhilaration.
Let your elevator and "exhilarator" soar.

Lighten up!
Laughter is STILL the best medicine. Seriously.

EN-Joy! Joy is an EN-side trip, not outside.
This is a fabulous journey. The Itinerary is divine!
And the Tour Guide is heavenly.

Smile. Often.

JUDGMENT

Form opinions and make decisions
based on wisdom, discernment, love
and understanding, or pass no judgment at all.

The verdict you pass on another,
measure for measure,
is the verdict you pass on yourself.

In general, opinions are formed and judgments
are made without any knowledge or consideration
of the "offender's" entire soul history.
Whatever you are witnessing, be assured,
it IS serving a higher purpose and apparently
a necessary step in the evolutionary plan
of the person or persons involved.

Avoid karmic imprisonment.
Practice the decree, "Judge not, lest you be judged."

JUSTICE

A sense of fairness and equity
is slowly, gently permeating hearts and minds
as consciousness is raised.

Awaken to the ancient sense of justness
and heed the call of impartiality.
The significance of being objective and neutral
in attitudes and opinions
will be validated in the new world order.

The Angel of Justice sleeps not.
Vindication of right is at hand.

Justice prevails!

KARMA

"Every cause has its effect; every effect has its cause;
everything happens according to Law;
Chance is but a name for Law not recognized;
there are many planes of causation,
but nothing escapes the Law." *

Guaranteed, you will reap what you sow.
Seeds planted, for better or worse, knowingly
or unknowingly, produce that which is inherent
in their core. Plant apple seeds, harvest apples.
Simple.

The same principle applies to our thoughts
and actions. Seeds of discord, chaos and confusion
reap havoc.
Kindness, compassion and goodness are the seeds
which yield a life replete with every joy.

Regardless of appearance, no one escapes this mighty
Cosmic Balancer. It is tempting to believe persons
have evaded the watchful eye of the Lord of Karma.
This couldn't be farther from the truth as the "Lord"
or "law" resides within the individual.

Karma is accrued whether we like it or not,
know it or not, or believe it or not!

Suffering from an overload of karmic debt?
Try Light.
The Law of Karma bows to the Law of Light!

* Hermetic Principle

LIGHT

"I AM THE LIGHT; I ALONE AM
WHAT I AM YOU ARE. YOU ARE THE LIGHT.
YOU ARE ONE WITH ME.
YOU MAY KNOW ME BY DESIRING TO KNOW ME.
TO KNOW ME IS TO BE ME. THROUGH MY LIGHT
ALONE CAN YOU KNOW ME.
YOU ARE LIGHT WHEN YOU KNOW
THAT YOU ARE LIGHT. YOU ARE ME
WHEN YOU KNOW THAT YOU ARE ME."

Light is the permeating, penetrating nucleus
of all that has ever been or ever will be created.
Light is ALL; all is LIGHT.

The darkness of ignorance is dissipated through
the tremendous power of Light. Simultaneously,
the soul is liberated from the anguish and monotony
of the wheel of karma.

Hold the Candle of Light firmly as the Force
moves through the soul providing illumination,
heightened sensitivity, and perception.

The Flame of Light will soon ignite
the hearts and minds of all beings
returning them once again to full knowledge of SELF.

* The Divine Iliad

LIMITLESSNESS

Appreciate yourself as Infinite, Immense and Endless.

Humankind forges chains of captivity,
not the Creator. As a soul reduces its scope
of Infiniteness by inviting fear and negativity to set the
parameters of the earth experience,
it suffers the consequences of desperation,
despondency or depression.

In past ages, up to and including yesterday,
ignorance of this law has wrought limitation.

Limitlessness echos through you;
all that is above is below -- IN YOU!

As a light being, the gift is yours to freely access
unlimited abundance, power,
love or anything you wish.

Good is your birthright.
Limit Liability; LOVE LIMITLESSLY!

LOVE

Love is your name.

You float endlessly in a Sea of Love.
Remember your name, Love, as you ride the crest
or sink helplessly to depths which are unfathomable.

You are not alone.
Love is caressing you.

MANIFESTATION

Demonstrate your Genius.

SEE, FEEL and KNOW your passion
waiting to burst forth.
Breathe life into matter;
allow your ideas to take shape.
Give Love expression!
What is within you deserves to be born.

Be precise.

Results are directly proportional
to the degree of focus and determination rendered.

Practice makes perfect.

MOMENTUM

Once the ball of thought or action gets rolling,
it gathers speed and power.

Momentum refers to the motion and force of energy
as it whirls into expression.

With the power of accumulated momentum of light
through the ages, there will be resurrected
within your consciousness the memory
of the powers which are yours to use
in expanding the borders of the Kingdom of Heaven.

NEUTRALIZATION

The power of Neutralization lies in its inherent ability
to nullify the effect of the pull of the pendulum
which swings you wildly from highs to lows,
agonies to ecstasies.
The soul acquires the grace to consciously polarize
itself at the point of stillness or rest
to regain poise and mental clarity.

Disturbing, discordant mood swings are rendered
ineffective as the soul overcomes the turbulent
forward/backward motion of its inner pendulum.
As difficulties are encountered, Neutralization
encourages the soul to distance itself
and rise above the turmoil.

NOTHING MOVES ME.

BE STILL.... AND KNOW.... I AM GOD

NON-
INTERFERENCE

The "I AM Presence" is firmly centered in all people,
all places and all things.
See it. Know it. Believe it.

Find and accept the good in everything and everyone.
Step back and allow others the divine privilege
of running their own lives.

Every individual knows its own truth.
The soul is embodied with the complete record
of its history and information regarding the path
it must walk.
Only highest good unfolds here. Trust.

This principle counsels - "MYOR"
(Mind Your Own Reality)

NONRESISTANCE

What you resist, persists!
Fighting fire with fire, produces more fire.
Resistance fosters a sense of separation,
thus diminishing and restricting
the natural flow of energy.

The Law of Nonresistance does not pit
force against force.
It implores the soul to incorporate nonviolence
as a way of life, relying on inner strength
to rise above adverse conditions.

Make the effort to operate with loving awareness
of your ONENESS with all life.

Nonresistance is irresistible.

OBEDIENCE

"To Thine Own Self be True."

The still, small voice you often hear
is none other than your God-Self
hoping to be honored.

How often have you moaned,
"I knew I should have..."
after you moved in the opposite direction
from the guidance you received.
Refusal to listen to the messages, direction
and guidance of the voice within is blatant
disobedience to your inner truth.
Conflict and turmoil are unleashed
which can take years or lifetimes to rectify.

Marching to your own music can be very challenging.
Marching to someone else's refrain
can be downright dangerous.
Only YOU have the whole truth for YOU within YOU.
Listen, trust and obey!

ONE

"I AM ONE GOD – and there is only ONE."
God is. And therein lies the dilemma
for human thought.
The problem with God is - God IS!
And, that's ALL there is!
There is nothing outside of this Force.
It is total, complete and singular.

Human beings argue and debate this "wholly" point,
becoming confused and lost in a maze of half truths,
all the while their sense of duality fostering feelings of
isolation and separateness.

In many instances, due to adherence to a faulty belief
system, we attempt to serve two gods,
a god of fear and God.
You can no longer afford to support belief systems
that insidiously infuse the soul
with fear, doubt and delusion.

"Keep your eye single." Serve ONE truth.
There is NOTHING outside the Presence.
Cherish your ONENESS.

PEACE

"No Peace lies in the future which is not hidden
in this present instant. Take Peace." *

Be satisfied with your life.

Reconcile your thoughts and feelings
with the awareness of God within.
Seek harmony by restoring the natural rhythm
of energy to body, mind and spirit.

Calmness and tranquillity have never abandoned you.

Infuse the Light of Peace into antagonistic ideas
or beliefs. Arguments or quarrels, no matter how
seemingly insignificant, disrupt the life stream;
hate severs the flow altogether.
The bitter seeds of war lie first within individual
consciousness, violating the sacred promise
to honor Peace.
The soul's chaos is then reflected outwardly
as a living nightmare.

Armistice Day has dawned; declare a truce.

Frater Giovanni

PERFECTION

The Essence of you IS Perfect.
It could be nothing less.

Beneath all apparent imperfection lies the REALITY,
"I AM WHOLE, COMPLETE AND PERFECT."

Your mission is to REALIZE and rediscover
your True Worth.

Helpful hint: Humility is the gateway to Perfection.

PERSEVERANCE

Perseverance is the "Keep on keeping on"
or "Don't quit" principle.

Any goal or vision requires the following:

Cultivate a strong WILL TO DO -- imperative.
Form a clear picture of what you wish to create.
Hold steadfastly to your vision
with LOVE until your creation materializes.
And, patience..... please!

A goal conceived is a goal achieved.

POLARITY

All manifested things have two sides, two aspects, two poles: a pair of opposites, with many degrees between the two extremes.*

Polarity is evidenced in such statements as "there are two sides to every coin" and "all truths are half truths." The difference between things seemingly diametrically opposed to each other is merely a matter of degree. Opposites may be reconciled.

Pairs of opposites exist everywhere upon examination into the deeper nature of anything.
Infinite Mind and finite mind are two poles of the same thing, their difference a matter of degree of vibration. Heat and cold, light and darkness, good and evil are opposite poles, identical in nature, separated only by degree of vibratory rate.

Material belonging to different classes cannot be transmuted into each other. Love, for example, cannot become East or West. That which is of the same class can have its polarity changed along the line of its inherent nature.
Love can be transmuted into hate and hatred can return to Love.

You can choose to raise or lower the thermostat at any time. Be the master of your mental states rather than the slave.

Hermetic Principle

POWER

You are a sovereign god
learning to effectively express your Power.
Act from an elevated position of strength and might
to produce your soul's delight.

In your soul memory, knowledge is stored of times
when you created star systems due to the tonal
quality of Power. You are free to resume work
of this caliber at any time; effort essential.

Out of ignorance, fear and innocence,
Power is often relinquished.
When you bestow the responsibility for your health,
well-being, happiness,
or life upon another individual,
you surrender Power.
Power shortages and outages are rampant
on the planet at this time.

Take command of your life!
Turn the electricity on.
The Power you generate will light up universes.

PRAISE

All creatures from the least to the greatest
are designed to give praise to the Creator.

Honor and applaud the Light within yourself;
it is then far easier to see the Light in others.
REALIZING the Light within and without
IS the Law of Praise.

It is All God. Bask in this simple truth.

Forget how to praise?
Sing! Dance! Laugh! Relax! Love!

PRESENT

BE

HERE

NOW!

There is absolutely NO energy
in the past or the future.

The wholeness of life is in THIS present moment.

Yesterday and tomorrow are illusions - at best.

PRODUCTION

Lights! Camera! Action!

You are the producer, director and star
of your own "Earthway" show.

Work on producing a star-spangled lifetime.

The Executive Producer has given the nod.

PURITY

Essence is completely pure, innocent
and flawlessly designed.
YOU are completely pure, innocent
and flawlessly designed.

Exonerate yourself from all thoughts which pollute
or taint your innocence.
Eliminate that which is no longer
for your Highest Good.

Guilt is a singularly contaminating force
which counters the Law of Purity.
Guilt is man-made second judging.
In your God Essence you are forever guiltless.

Scrub up. Clean house. Remove any scarlet lettering.

REALIZATION

Realization - you finally actualize
what you always knew.

YOU ARE GOD IN DRAG. Get Real.

REBIRTH

You are a wave in the Ocean of Life.
In the mystery of your inner rhythm,
you pull back from the shore
and the wave folds itself into the ocean
only to gain renewed strength and energy
to splash once more upon Its shores.

Birth is your unfolding,
death is the enfolding.
Love is the Ocean.

REINCARNATION

You are CREATED free and equal,
but you are not BORN so.
The Law of Reincarnation resolves the seeming
iniquities that exist among people. Known as the
"cycle of necessity" and the "door of liberation",
this law enables the immortal soul to take another
form to continue its learning process.
Reincarnation teaches equal opportunities for all
and special privileges for none, success being
the reward for work well done and failure the penalty
of indolence. Work left unfinished today
will be picked up tomorrow.

Every individual is exactly where they have earned
the right to be. Cause and effect rule the universe,
there is no blind chance.

All types of experience are offered and lessons
garnered as the soul enacts various roles in the
human drama. Any situation that has knowingly
or unknowingly been thrown out of balance
must be corrected.

Only love alleviates the necessity
for another earth experience.

Record numbers of Light Beings are choosing
to incarnate at this time to help heal the planet
with their Limitless Love.

It is a privilege to be here now.

RELAXATION

STOP THE ACTION AND JUST BE!

Come into a more perfect state of being
by simply Being!
Allow the physical, mental and spiritual bodies
to be still.
Surrender your finer, subtler bodies to quietude.
Become a pure channel for creative energy.

On the seventh day God rested.
(Seven symbolizes a measure of completion
and perfection).
As gods in the discovery stage,
it is crucial to discern points of closure,
be they major or minor.
These junctures should be honored with stillness
in proportion to the energy expended.

Respect your need for a balanced flow
of activity and rest.

RESTORATION

The soul, as a magnificent work of art,
undergoes constant Restoration.

Dirt and grime must be removed from the canvas.

Your true colors ache to explode
in a burst of brilliance.

The Illuminating One has palette in hand,
ever rejuvenating the inherent beauty
of this divine masterpiece - YOU.

"Behold, I make all things new."

RETRIBUTION

All beings come to earth with an inborn
code of ethics.
NO ONE arrives without this guidance system,
regardless of appearance.

When an individual violates their code of goodness
and consciously chooses to harm another life form,
at that very instant they set in motion
the Law of Retribution.
The soul cannot help but suffer the consequences
of its condemnation and lack of love.

The day of making amends and restitution
WILL dawn!

REVERENCE

Honor ALL life.

Everything is sacred.

RHYTHM

"Everything flows, out and in;
everything has its tides;
all things rise and fall.
The pendulum-swing manifests in everything.
The measure of the swing to the right
is the measure of the swing to the left;
rhythm compensates." *

All things evolve and resolve. A life begins, a life ends.
Inflow, outflow; building up and tearing down;
creation and recreation - ever unfolding
in perfect meter.

As one facet of life ebbs,
increase is simultaneously experienced
in another sector.
Loss may be sustained, a job may disintegrate,
a partner may leave,
yet another door opens to allow further growth.

Ebb and flow is NOT designed as an exercise
in depression. Release frustration, bitterness
or regret during low tide.

Trust the guiding hand of the Universal Force,
the Power within the pendulum.

* Hermetic Principle

RIGHTEOUSNESS

You were given power and dominion over all things.
Be a loyal caretaker.

"Right-use-ness" is the just and proper application and
use of everything in your stewardship while visiting
this planet.

Nothing actually belongs to you on this sojourn
to earth.

As guardian, you agreed to use your gifts and talents
wisely.

SELF-PRESERVATION

Constructively nurture and develop body, mind
and spirit. As you benefit, all life is enhanced —
even to the farthest star system.

Altruism and selfishness are opposite ends
of the same pole.
Self-Preservation calls for walking the middle road.

Self-sacrifice serves no purpose.
This is not to be confused with self-denial
or conscious choice to curb or eliminate
self-centeredness.

Body, mind and spirit are designed to function
as an integrated, healthy unit.
Depleting any of these bodies to the point of
bankruptcy impedes the realization process.

(Remember, it was your choice to take a body.)
Honor it.

SIMPLICITY

Unclog and un-clutter your thoughts and feelings.

LOVE LIFE. BE HAPPY.

K I S S.
(Keep It Souly Simple)

H U G.

SUCCESS

The road to Success is constantly under construction.
As you are laying the pavement,
trust the road will wind toward Home.

Boulders and barriers may greet you along the way.
Remove them one by one and good fortune
will be your companion.

If you are facing an insurmountable road block,
the signs are indicating it is time
for an attitude adjustment.

Work steadily toward completion of your roadway,
but construct with joy. This is Success.

SUPPLY

The storehouse is eternally full.

Supply IS endless and limitless.

Life is a tireless, generous Giver,
consistently recognizing and meeting all needs.

SYMMETRY

As the breathtaking beauty of a flawless tapestry
is delicately formed by the intertwining
of each glorious thread to create the whole,
so it is with Life.

The balanced interrelationship of all parts
constitutes a magnificent whole.

SYNCHRONISM

Synchronism represents the principle of two
or more identical circumstances
operating in unison and occurring at the same time.

What may appear to be coincidence is, in fact,
the full expression of this law linking and entwining
energy with like energy.

Expand awareness of interplay with other dimensions
and realities.

Parallel universes and simultaneous existences
await your exploration.

THANKSGIVING

In all things give Thanks.

From the center of your being,
croon a ceaseless song of gratitude.
The melody will be heard throughout the kingdom
as it ascends on the wings of Love
to fulfill your deepest desire.

Open your heart. Sing out!

Gifts are sometimes cleverly disguised
as challenges or obstacles.
Double up on gratitude. Sing louder.

Remember, in the heart of the coal is a diamond.

Alleluia!

THOUGHT

All thought is a projection of energy from
the One Still Light of Universal Mind.

Thought proceeds and governs
ALL forms of manifestation.

Whatever is adhered to in thought or emotion
WILL come into existence.

The result of your thinking indelibly stamps itself
upon the universal substance in and around you.
Put some thought behind your thinking!

Dare to "mine your mind";
your world needs the gold.

TRANSFIGURATION

As this age of Light unfolds, the soul will become
adept at radiating energy and light
from within to such an intense degree
that the physical body will change appearance
and become glorified.

Twelve major vortexes of energy
are activated and stimulated simultaneously
during Transfiguration.

The pitch of energy is so high that the body
becomes a radiating, pulsating field of Light.

This is Ascension.

Love is how it is accomplished.

TRANSFORMATION

To change is to live,
to change often is to live divinely!

Fundamental restructuring is necessary.
The hour has come to shift your conscious awareness
and discard the mantel of ignorance.

Degree by degree, thought by thought,
re-formation is essential.

Fear must be transmuted into faith,
chaos into calm, ill health into wholeness,
hatred into love.
Yes, even karma may be transformed by Light.

Wave your Magic Wand;
turn into your Higher Self.

TRUST

God trusts you.
If you would rely on yourself,
you would trust you too.

Your highest good is ALWAYS unfolding,
regardless of outer appearances.

Believe in the Plan!

UNITY

In a prism, no facet is more beautiful
nor more perfect than the next.

Each is distinctively exquisite;
appearing as many, emanating all colors,
it is ONE.

You are an individual ray of the prism,
and you are the entire prism.

Iridescent Radiance shimmers Her Light — uniting all.

VIBRATION

Everything moves, vibrates and circles.
Nothing is completely at rest.

The All is in a state of constant vibration
so intense It virtually appears to slumber.

The difference among life forms is due entirely
to the varying rate of vibration
found in each unique expression of life.

Thoughts and emotions,
have a vibratory pattern as well.

As energy is released, it affects the minds
of other persons. Be discerning about picking up
someone's "vibes."

Be equally careful of what you are dispersing
into the universe.
Your vibrations are sensed in the farthest star system.

Lighten up.
Shift your vibratory rate by elevating your thoughts.
This is the way to bring heaven to earth.

Do it.

VISUALIZATION

The completed design of that which you yearn
to bring forth resides in a cocoon-like,
flawless state of perfection, deep in the sanctuary
of your own heart and soul.

Breathe life into your desires.
Give form to the children of your mind.

Collective consciousness has determined
creations are outside and separate from themselves.
Faulty thinking has resulted in frustration
and difficulty in bringing ideas to fruition.

"En-vision" perfect creations.
See it whole, complete and perfect IN you.

Then, project it on to the screen of life.

WISDOM

The path of Wisdom is simple.

Seek to learn of your God-Self.

Then be It.

Author Notes

For as long as I can remember, I believed deeply in the presence of God as a motivating, moving force of my life. I have a simple faith and an even simpler trust in the Divine Plan. These are tremendous gifts for which I am deeply grateful.

I seek diligently to pay attention and follow Direction. Laughingly, I proclaim, " I take direction well." Direction from the Boss, that is. Thus, I believe this book came to be born. This work is a sacred responsibility undertaken with humility, humor and light.

May the Spirit of these words touch you as deeply as they touched me while bringing them to life.